Maine Sail

Maine Sail

AN ARTIST'S JOURNAL OF A CRUISE DOWN EAST

by Margaret S. McCrea

DOWN EAST BOOKS · CAMDEN, MAINE

COVER DESIGN AND INTERIOR PAGES
Lurelle Cheverie - Camden, Maine

Printed in China. RPS

5   4   3   2   1

Down East Books
A division of Down East Enterprise, Inc.,
Publisher of *Down East*, the Magazine of Maine

Book orders: 1-800-685-7962
www.downeastbooks.com

CREDITS

Hank and Jan Taft, Curtis Rindlaub.
A Cruising Guide to the Maine Coast, third edition.
Peaks Island, Me.: Diamond Pass Publishing, Inc., 2002.
Whenever we cruise in Maine, this guide is our chief
source of local knowledge in our explorations.

National Oceanic and Atmospheric Administration (NOAA) Charts,
National Ocean Service, United States Department of Commerce

For my loving husband and captain, Peter,
who continually tries to keep me focused and on course.
Without him, my journals would lack adventure.

With appreciation to

my Mom and Dad for a lifetime of support and encouragement;

my friends and collectors for their generous support;

and Down East Books for believing in my vision.

Contents

Belfast
Searsport

Castine

Blue Hill

Lincolnville
Islesboro

Cape
Rosier

Camden
Rockport

EAST
PENOBSCOT
BAY

FRENCHMAN
BAY

Thomaston

Rockland

North Haven

Deer Isle

BLUE HILL
BAY

Mount
Desert
Island

Bar
Harbor

Southwest
Harbor

Northeast
Harbor

Vinalhaven

JERICHO
BAY

Swans Island

Schoodic
Point

WEST
PENOBSCOT
BAY

ISLE AU HAUT
BAY

Isle au Haut

Campobello
Island

West
Quoddy
Head

Machias

ENGLISHMAN
BAY

Roque
Island

MACHIAS
BAY

Cutler

PLEASANT
BAY

Jonesport

Petit
Manan
Point

Great
Wass
Island

Grand
Manan

Introduction

Maine Sail is an illustrated journal describing an unhurried cruise along the coast of Maine. It is modeled on and drawn from my daily journals and personal observations made over the course of many sailing trips, but in *Maine Sail,* highlights from several journals have been combined into one archetypal late-summer cruise down east. References to specific dates or times have been omitted to help the reader escape any feeling of schedule or deadline—just as happens while cruising. On the water, life is at a different pace in a different place.

My husband, Peter, and I have cruised on *Panacea* for the past fifteen years, living aboard for as much as fifteen months at a time in foreign waters or as little as a weekend in a nearby Maine island anchorage. The boat is our home during these periods when we exist as waterborne nomads—rarely staying in the same location for more than a few days at a time, choosing different ports and anchorages depending on our mood. Time and how it is spent are within our control. We become in tune with our senses and the environment, experiencing a gentle sea breeze or a full-blown gale with heightened awareness, just as we do the call of a loon and the scents of salt air and pine. Thoughts and observations formulate without interruption, allowing ideas full opportunity to crystallize.

Having waxed philosophical over the aforementioned, I have to acknowledge that I do not settle into the cruising life effortlessly. One of the most difficult aspects of embarking upon an extended cruise and making it happen is disconnecting oneself from land. Not only must one have a capable boat and skipper and everything necessary to maintain daily living aboard, but plans must be put in place to handle personal affairs in one's absence. In our case, I am not a planner. My preference (and style) is to take each day at a time, each hour at a time. Left to me, our extended cruises could never happen. Peter, however, is a planner. He *makes* it happen. He prods me into action, navigates our vessel, monitors the weather and tides, and plots a safe course.

We never bring a cell phone aboard. The intrusion would defeat the purpose of the cruise. By our definition, a cruise means escaping that which usually consumes life when ashore. Within a few hours of departure, pressing schedules and other demands are left in our wake and soon forgotten. Only that which is truly essential remains: a sound hull below, with ample water beneath the keel; a good mate; a steady breeze and cooperative weather; beautiful islands; and the scenic Maine coastline as far as the eye can see.

This is cruising—cruising in Maine. Cruising at its finest.

During our cruises, I settle into the rhythm of life at sea.

I lose track of previous concerns.

Constantly changing conditions and scenery provide a stream of images.

My brain is like a spider's web, catching thoughts and

images to be stored away in tiny cocoons for future nourishment.

SAINT GEORGE RIVER AND WEST PENOBSCOT BAY

Saint George River and
West Penobscot Bay

Departure day. Gorgeous weather…
cool breeze, low humidity, mid-70s. …
It doesn't come any better. We dinghy
from Thomaston's town landing on the
St. George River and board *Panacea* for
an extended cruise along the coast
and islands of down east Maine.

The wind is dead on the nose, so we motor downriver, rather than raise sail.
The upper river is too narrow for tacking, and we are eager to get away. As
we near the lower reaches of the river, in Cushing, we are envious of a
graceful Friendship sloop under full sail.

Today, our first day, is a short run. We nip into Maple Juice Cove
for the evening, allowing me time to catch my breath. My captain
is like a fish returning to sea, while I agonize over things I
might have forgotten to take care of, forgotten to tell someone,
or forgotten to pack. No matter the planning or preparations,
I am never quite ready to leave our land home behind.

Once we're anchored inside the cove, I look
aft up the gradual rise from shore to the steep, proud
lines of Christina Olson's house, made famous by the
masterful brush of Andrew Wyeth. The structure's
massive proportions, in darkened and rough
weathered clapboards, are viewed in miniature from our vantage point. Five minutes
after the anchor is down, my eye chases lines
with a pencil, which are quickly colored
with late-afternoon purple and gold.

16

Before sunset, we jump in the dinghy,
our water taxi, for a tour along the
shore and a peek at the local architecture.

There Sits a House in Maple Juice Cove
that Speaks to Me of Maine

Southern Island Lobster Maze, Tenants Harbor

We awoke this morning to a heavy sky. Three guillemots, busy little sea birds that look like bathtub ducks, splash and fuss around the boat. They pay no mind to weather. Dark colored with two white spots on their wings and bright red feet, they repeatedly pop in and out of the water like corks as they dive and feed below us.

Although it's dismal and foggy, there is enough breeze to raise sail. The white shape of Marshall Point lighthouse in Port Clyde takes form to port as we sail under the tip of the St. George peninsula.

Skirting around Southern Island brings us into the protected reaches of Tenants Harbor, where lobster buoys are so thick we could walk to shore. Fog slips in and out. Its gauzy veil lifts briefly to allow a quick sketch of some lobster boats remaining on their moorings today.

Ashore, a lunch of lobster stew and mussels at Cod End takes the edge off our appetites, and a leisurely walk to a local quarry stretches our legs. On our return to the harbor, it is thick o' fog—a very apt description used by old-timers. We settle in for the evening, hoping forecasts for improved conditions in the morning are correct.

19

The following morning remains sunless. Fog hovers in the form of low clouds, but land has vaguely reappeared around the harbor. With anchor hoisted, we weave our way to sea, heading northeast up Muscle Ridge Channel through a floating latticework of lobster buoys. The surface is flat calm, interrupted only by an occasional ripple of wind. The sea swallows our twisted track around the lobster buoy slalom as fog ruffles layer in bands. Floating spruce tips are suspended in mid-air, the islands below obliterated from view.

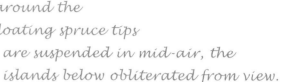

To port sits the neat little cluster of Whitehead Light and its outbuildings, one of the few unpainted lighthouse towers on the coastline.

The lobster pots begin to thin. At one point, they were so thick I could see no passage through them.

The understated Owls Head Light appears to port.

20

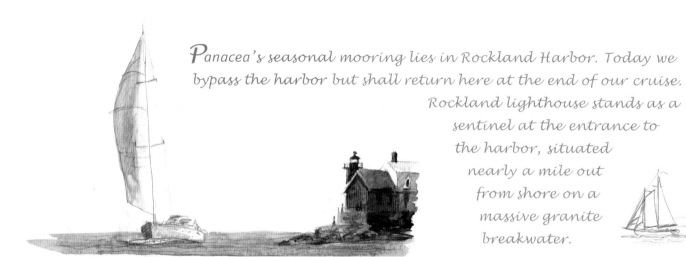

Panacea's seasonal mooring lies in Rockland Harbor. Today we bypass the harbor but shall return here at the end of our cruise. Rockland lighthouse stands as a sentinel at the entrance to the harbor, situated nearly a mile out from shore on a massive granite breakwater.

Visitors exerting the effort to hike the entire length of the breakwater are rewarded with a feeling of being at sea, windjammers sailing within feet of where they stand on the light keeper's balcony.

We duck into Rockport Harbor for a close-up view of the lighthouse on Indian Island. Although now privately owned, it remains a picturesque landmark visible to sailors and landlubbers alike.

margaret a mc crea

A lone lobsterman works the area, methodically pulling his color-coded buoys attached by a line (referred to as pot warp) to a string of pots lying on the ocean floor.

The buoy displayed above his deckhouse indicates his registered color combination as solid red-orange with no creative (or time-consuming) striping detail applied.

23

Keeper's House, Curtis Island

24

Continuing northward,
we parallel the shoreline
where blue hills merge
with blue sea.

Always a favorite, Curtis
Island's red-roofed keeper's
house next catches my eye.
Shapes and angles change
quickly even at the slow pace of a sailboat
making 4 or 5 knots. Situated on the seaward
side of the island, this picturesque lighthouse
is best viewed from the water.

Secured to a floating dock for
the night in Camden's inner harbor,
we watch an active summer
day come to a close.

Angelique

Appledore

Mary Day

Schooners in Maine's windjammer fleet continue to ply Maine waters. In their former years, these coasters were the 18-wheelers of the sea, carrying cargo to ports of the North Atlantic.

Although today's passengers experience a kinder version of life aboard, the sounds in the rigging, the environmental elements, and the smell of the sea remain the same. Guests are provided with a picture of Maine not viewed from any scenic highway.

One by one the day boats return, their human cargo wearing a day of sun and wind on their faces. Windjammer masts tower above the lookout monument atop the imposing hulk of Mt. Battie, hovering behind the harbor. Darkness comes quickly as the sun sinks behind the slumbering Camden Hills to the west.

26

Penobscot Bay *Andante*

During dinner last night, friends offered to drive us to
the top of Mt. Battie. At the summit this morning, we climb
the stone tower (a miniature replica of the Old Stone
Mill in Newport, Rhode Island), which appears as
but a nubbin from the harbor below. Spread
before us is a panoramic vista of Penobscot
Bay. To the north and east, we see Islesboro
and beyond to Cape Rosier and Deer Isle.
Blue Hill is just a small bump on the
far-distant horizon. To the southeast
lie North Haven and Vinalhaven, with
Isle au Haut beyond, and to the south and
west lie Owls Head, Matinicus, and Monhegan.
A veritable banquet of images collect in my mental web.

Not yet ready to return to the boat,
we hike the back road from Camden
into Rockport, viewing the white-
girdled Belted Galloways en route.

Being a farmer's granddaughter, I never tire of
seeing these resident bovines, stark graphic patterns
of black on white in lush pastoral settings. I wonder
if they ever tire of being viewed as curiosities?

Returning to Camden while there is
still daylight, we dinghy to Curtis Island.
Now I have the opportunity to sketch the
lighthouse lines from land—a real treat.

29

Tree on Sherman Point

On our exit from the harbor the next morning, we take the passage by Northeast Point, leaving a nest for three at daymark 3 to starboard. Ospreys find stationary navigation aids to be sound supports for their gangly stick-and-twig-style nests. Six watchful eyes peer down as we ghost by, following our transit until we no longer seem a threat.

We pass the schooner Mercantile, her sails set but using power assist since there is little wind.

An unhurried sail up the bay takes us along the western shores of Islesboro and into one of its protected anchorages. Margaret Chase Smith, the ferry running between Lincolnville and the island, crosses our bow on a course to the Grindel Point ferry landing.

Soon after passing the landing, we pick up a mooring belonging to friends who live on Broad Cove. Later, a trip ashore to the town landing allows a brisk walkabout and a small, hasty watercolor of Grindel Point lighthouse.

Moosequito

We walk smartly, dodging and swatting the many mosquitoes that are having their feeding frenzy at this time of day. Due to their size, I note that an additional O belongs in their name.

Grindel Point, Islesboro

31

This morning, as we get under way, the ferry resumes its scheduled transits to and from the mainland.

We backtrack west toward the mainland and the compact little hillside town of Belfast. The harbor is colorful with a cluster of bright red tugs tied alongside old sheds and buildings, resistant survivors of redevelopment. It is visually pleasing to see old waterfronts still bearing a few remnants from the past, unique character snippets of their former personalities.

We tie briefly to the short-term visitors' dock. Peter makes a run to the supermarket for provisions while I do journal duty.

On Peter's return, a short motor trip north takes us into Searsport for an afternoon visit to the interesting and informative maritime museum. It would seem that Searsport and Thomaston have an ongoing bragging contest over who had the most sea captains during the nineteenth century.

A wide tidal range makes for ladder landings of Mt. Everest proportions.

Tugboats in Belfast

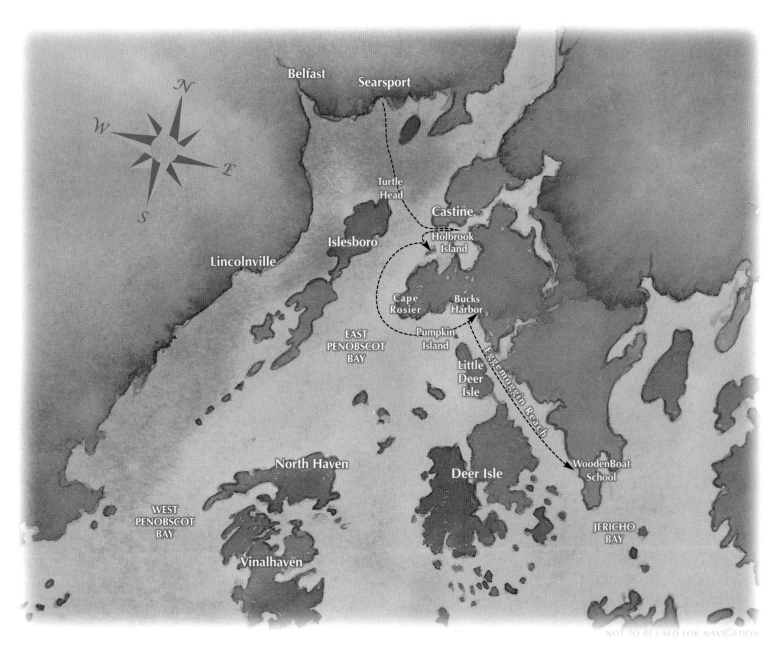

EAST PENOBSCOT BAY AND EGGEMOGGIN REACH

Belfast

Searsport

N
W
S
E

Turtle Head

Castine

Islesboro

Holbrook Island

Lincolnville

Cape Rosier

Bucks Harbor

EAST PENOBSCOT BAY

Pumpkin Island

Little Deer Isle

Eggemoggin Reach

North Haven

Deer Isle

WoodenBoat School

WEST PENOBSCOT BAY

JERICHO BAY

Vinalhaven

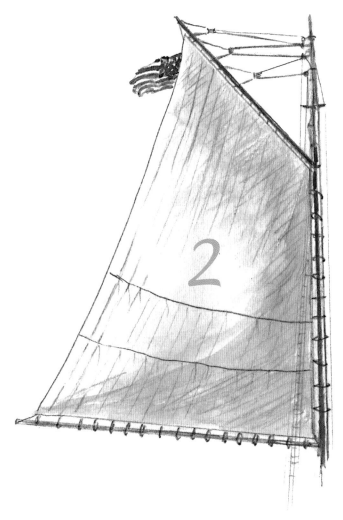

2

East Penobscot Bay and
Eggemoggin Reach

Today we awake to flat, calm seas in Searsport Harbor. Although the lack of breeze was nice for sleeping last night, it does not make for good sailing this morning. We motor southeastward, passing to the north of Islesboro's Turtle Head.

At the entrance into the Bagaduce River at Castine, Dice Head Light lies to port, nestled in a sea of inky black-green conifers.

A short distance beyond, we drop anchor opposite the large Maine Maritime Academy training ship. A short dinghy ride across the channel takes us to the town dock. Nearby Eaton's Boatyard, its main building identified by weathered red shingles, is definitely one of Castine's rich character snippets. After a walkabout along streets lined with solid Yankee architecture, we return to the boat.

A frontal passage is forecast and we are quite exposed, so we move around to the protection and solitude of a cove off Holbrook Island, below Castine. As we sit in a tranquil cockpit just before sunset, a bald eagle appears and silently swoops to the uppermost section of a massive spruce. He is immediately harassed by a self-righteous, territorial seagull. Blatantly ignoring the disgruntled gull, the eagle diligently perches until he snatches his prey from the water below. Following a leisurely beach picnic of sushi, he quietly disappears from the scene. It would seem that territorial disputes are not limited to great nations.

The next day, we awake to torrents of rain filling the sea. We hunker down with Scrabble and good books. A great day for the parched Maine landscape; we hear audible sighs of relief from the islands around us as they plump before our eyes, soaking up moisture like sponges.

Yesterday's frontal passage brings clear weather today. Following breakfast in a sparkling rain-washed cockpit, we enjoy a comfortable southerly broad reach along the western and southern shores of Cape Rosier, taking an easterly heading into the waters leading up into Eggemoggin Reach. Bay islands abound.

Approaching bell buoy ER, Hog Island and Fiddle Head border our starboard horizon as Cape Rosier falls behind.

One of several highlights of Eggemoggin Reach is impeccable Pumpkin Island, lying off the northwest tip of Little Deer Isle. Truly a designer island, it has all the right accents: perfectly proportioned light tower and attached cape-style cottage, a smattering of malachite-green conifers spiking skyward, and a boathouse growing from granite roots. All this with ocean frontage and an unparalleled view of the Camden Hills to the west. Sketches of this lighthouse lover's epitome fly from my pencil as we skim by. There simply are no unflattering angles.

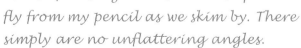

As we prepare to anchor for the night in nearby Bucks Harbor, windjammers from every point of the compass meander into the glow of a magnificent pumpkin-colored sunset, the atmosphere bathed in a yellow-peach wash.

Pumpkin Sunset

We share an evening anchorage nestled amongst an orderly but tightly packed fleet. Fog rolls in with an accompanying chill, and we hunker down below for the evening.

As we climb into the cockpit the next morning, smoke rises from the schooners' cook-stoves and mingles with the remaining dawn mist. Reflections on an inky sea-green carpet stretch and blend into shore. A hazy sun starts to burn through, with promise of yet another perfect day.

We are intrigued by a stately old New England-style house high on a hill with a view to the sea. We hike up the highway for a closer look. The gentleman we meet in the yard invites us into his home—formerly his grandfather's—where he shares memories of a rich and full life.

40

A stop at the grocery store deli to pick up lunch and a few groceries is always a Bucks Harbor highlight. At the captain's request, we also swing by the marina and invite a couple of lobsters for dinner.

Bucks Harbor Grocery

The following day turns into one of those crisp, see-forever days.
No schedule, and all day to get wherever we might be when we drop sail.

Sailing down
Eggemoggin Reach,
we pass J & E Riggin,
still raising sail.

We tuck into the lee of
Torrey Island for a
lunch break. The vivid little island is a mass of
greens, punctuated by a cluster of bright magenta
and pink wildflowers.

Although purple loosestrife
is not a particularly popular
species, due to its invasive
characteristics, one has to
admire its brilliant, notice-
me color. I dutifully pay it
homage in my sketch book.

Our evening anchorage is in the protected harbor off the
WoodenBoat School where, by day's end, we are surrounded
by a total of fifteen windjammers. Without planning, we
have become witnesses to their annual Windjammer Day.

42

Dropping Sail

We watch in awe as each vessel purposefully rounds up into the wind, released sails dropping to the decks like huge, fluttering birds. At sunset a bagpiper pipes mournful strains of "Amazing Grace." Flags are lowered and guests speak in hushed tones. Although strangers, everyone shares something intangible.

43

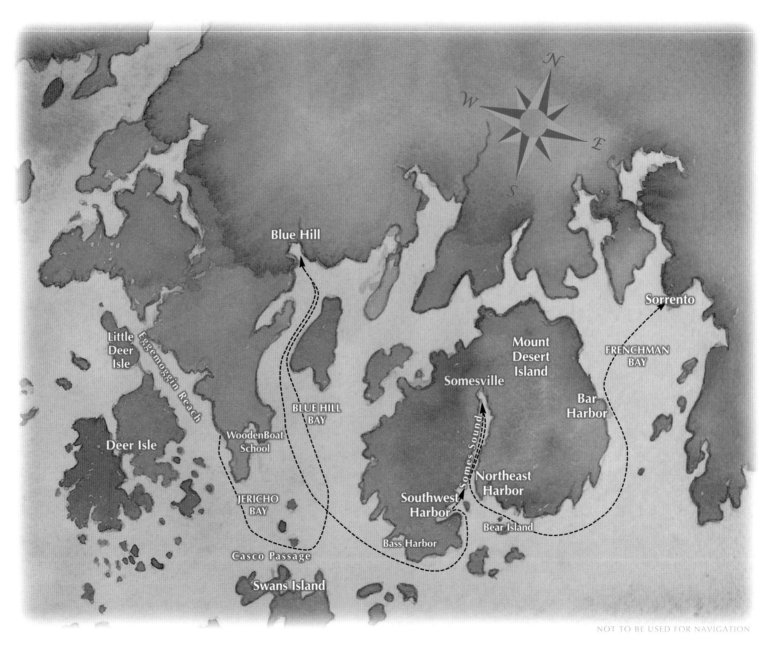

Little
Deer
Isle

Eggemoggin Reach

Blue Hill

Sorrento

Deer Isle

BLUE HILL
BAY

WoodenBoat
School

Mount
Desert
Island

Somesville

FRENCHMAN
BAY

Bar
Harbor

JERICHO
BAY

Northeast
Harbor

Southwest
Harbor

Bear Island

Casco Passage

Bass Harbor

Swans Island

JERICHO BAY, BLUE HILL BAY, MOUNT DESERT ISLAND, AND FRENCHMAN BAY

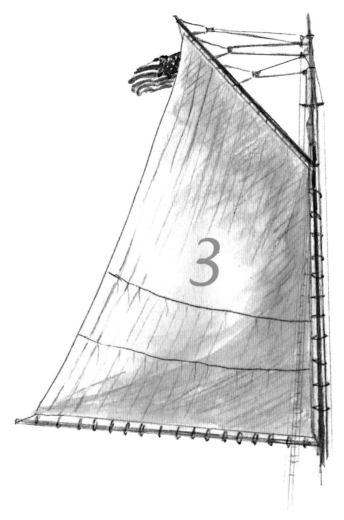

Jericho Bay, Blue Hill Bay,
Mount Desert Island, and Frenchman Bay

Come morning, we continue our journey around the islands on our cruise to nowhere in no hurry.

After negotiating the marked channel through Casco Passage at the south-east end of Eggemoggin Reach, we decide to turn northward and head into Blue Hill Harbor.

We find anchoring to be tight, so we pick up a Kollegewidgwok Yacht Club mooring. Love that name—Kollegewidgwok—which, we are told, is derived from an early Native American reference to saltwater falls.

A dinghy ride into the village dock confirms that landing will only be possible at mid- to high tide. We learn this the hard way upon our return, when we have to heft the dinghy over rocks to reach the water. I mutter about navigational shortcomings.

We enjoy this pretty little town for a couple of days, exploring and sketching where the blue hill meets the green sea. The lighting varies as the sun bumps clouds overhead, changing dark blue-black patches into yellow-green. In the evenings, Blue Hill lives up to its name and morphs into a deep shade of blue.

The next day, friends from nearby Surry lead us on a hike up Blue Hill. Hard to believe this is the same little blue bump we observed from Camden a few days ago—now we strain to see Mt. Battie. We enjoy a great walk along a gradual incline through blueberry barrens. At a false top we pause for a view, then continue climbing through a shaded passage under thick spruce boughs, blotting out the sun. A carpeted pathway of russet and sienna pine needles takes us to the crest, where we are bathed in clear, pristine air. Climbing a fire tower at the summit completes our ascent. What cannot be adequately captured on film or in sketches is tucked into my web.

Peekaboo fog for most of the day. Before our departure, Peter runs errands while I watch yacht club sailing instructors teach young sailors the rudiments of rowing and teamwork. Two lessons in one, no doubt memorable ones.

49

After taking on ice and settling our bill with the yacht club, we turn into the heavy mist, which eventually clears as the sun burns through. Passing Blue Hill Bay lighthouse on Green Island to starboard, we peer through a milky film to see cast shadows on the keeper's house, hinting at clearing air to westward.

Blue Hill Bay Light in the Fog

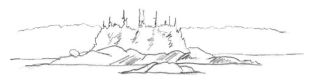

Orono Island

Leaving Blue Hill Bay, we enter a different day. Improving visibility reveals layers of islands as far as the eye can see—nearly as abundant as the layers of lobster buoys we constantly dodge.

Asa Island

As we continue, a small cloud puff hovers between the sun and the mountains below, creating a dark, round shadow blob... eye candy. Looking around, we see little evidence of human habitation. All is wilderness and water, as yet permanently touched by Nature alone.

The Swans Island ferry passes on its regular run between islands.

Bass Harbor Head looms off the port bow, angles constantly changing as we pass. Such a spectacular lighthouse is rooted there, its brilliant white outline gleaming against salmon-colored cliffs embedded with clumps of dark green.

52

As we move through the buoyed channel over the bar, we sail with the light close abeam. We're in good company: Victory Chimes joins us on this scenic route.

Victory Chimes off Bass Harbor Light

We breeze into Southwest Harbor on Mount Desert Island, the dramatic spectacle of the island's mountains spread in an expansive blue panorama before us.

Sailing up Somes Sound, Maine's spectacular fiord, is an incredibly peaceful experience. A combination of cliffs and pastoral settings line the deep channel leading into Somesville.

Anchorage in the protected cul-de-sac at the top of the sound offers 360 degrees of impressive scenery. We dinghy ashore for a walkabout and bookstore fix. Overlooking Mill Pond, we find a solitary bench and enjoy the view of a mountain dome to the southeast.

While we are ashore, the schooner Heritage slips in and anchors below Panacea.

Mirror of Friendship

While we are sitting in the cockpit after dinner, a graceful Friendship sloop vies for our attention as she flirtatiously sashays on a nearby mooring.

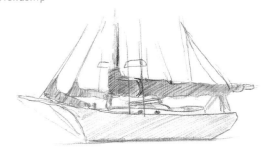

Peregrine

Reluctantly, we leave this absolute peacefulness behind. However, we have learned that when cruising in Maine, no matter how beautiful or serene the anchorage one is departing, there is always another not far away.

A solitary seagull impassively observes from a nearby mooring ball as we exit this scenic hideaway. Eagle Cliff rises to starboard, and two eagles soar on air currents high above.

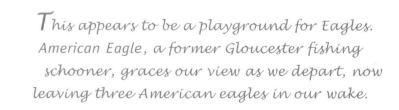

This appears to be a playground for Eagles. American Eagle, a former Gloucester fishing schooner, graces our view as we depart, now leaving three American eagles in our wake.

American Eagle off Mount Desert Island

Black Jack, a sloop based in Northeast Harbor, heads out on an early morning charter, her large white sail boldly contrasting against her dark hull and brightwork. To starboard, a power boat is taken out on a test run in the protected waters near Greening Island, off Southwest Harbor.

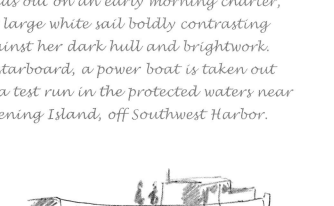

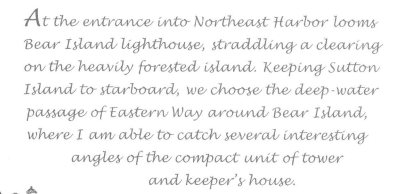

At the entrance into Northeast Harbor looms Bear Island lighthouse, straddling a clearing on the heavily forested island. Keeping Sutton Island to starboard, we choose the deep-water passage of Eastern Way around Bear Island, where I am able to catch several interesting angles of the compact unit of tower and keeper's house.

Bear Island Lighthouse

Lighthouses almost seem to have conflicting personalities. They are like Sirens. The beauty and romance associated with them call us in for a closer view, but, by design, they are there to warn us to stand clear.

Lobster boats are nearly as numerous as the pots being pulled.

Goia sails along the Seal Harbor shoreline, an impressive silhouette against an even more impressive backdrop.

Shifty fog descends, leaving the rest of the day's passage in limited visibility. After a Bar Harbor sail-by, seeing very little of the waterfront and its ghosted fleet of boats, we sail across Frenchman Bay. Although we see no other boats, we hear numerous air-horn blasts all afternoon.

Fog lifts on cue as we near Sorrento Harbor, where we pick up a wooden mooring float into which has been carved "In memory of Robert M. Lewis, 1886-1958. He cruised." A touching gesture for a gentleman sailor. How I would love to hear his stories.

60

From the mooring, we look past the tip of Dram Island to starboard, across a now crystal clear Frenchman Bay, to the dramatic outline of Cadillac Mountain. Thank you for sharing your impressive view, Mr. Lewis.

A walk along the shoreline reveals many interestingly shaped stones on the beach. Peter finds a striated arrowhead lying below the tide line. How long has it tumbled in the sea?

After purchasing lobster from a local fisherman, we jump in his pickup for a ride back to the harbor. Trying to make conversation, I naively ask, "Have you lived here all your life?" He drolly responds, "Not yet."

61

Sorrento

Petit
Manan
Light

Shipstern
Island

Nash
Island

Pot Rock

Great
Wass
Island

Jonesport

Roque
Island

Head Harbor
Island

Libby
Islands

Cutler

Little
Island
Light

West
Quoddy
Head

Head
Harbour

Campobello
Island

Grand
Manan

N
W   E
S

DOWN EAST TO CAMPOBELLO ISLAND, NEW BRUNSWICK

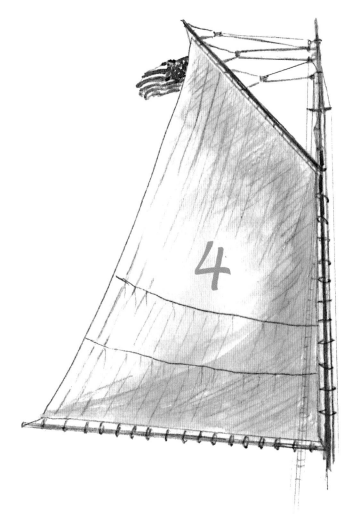

Down East to
Campobello Island, New Brunswick

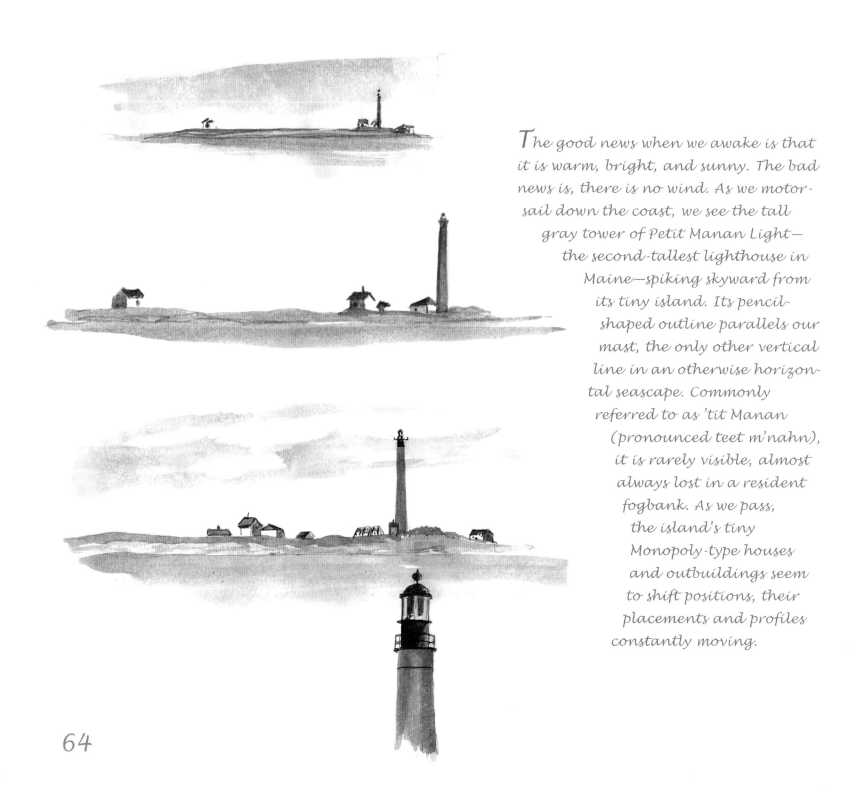

The good news when we awake is that it is warm, bright, and sunny. The bad news is, there is no wind. As we motor-sail down the coast, we see the tall gray tower of Petit Manan Light—the second-tallest lighthouse in Maine—spiking skyward from its tiny island. Its pencil-shaped outline parallels our mast, the only other vertical line in an otherwise horizontal seascape. Commonly referred to as 'tit Manan (pronounced teet m'nahn), it is rarely visible, almost always lost in a resident fogbank. As we pass, the island's tiny Monopoly-type houses and outbuildings seem to shift positions, their placements and profiles constantly moving.

Shipstern Island

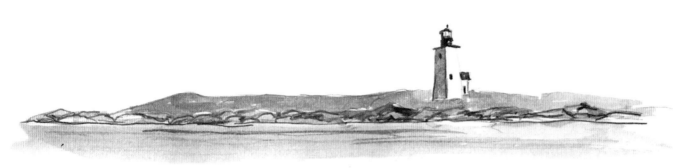

Nash Island

Shipstern and Nash islands are easily defined landmarks in the bay, soon followed by Pot Rock, which actually does resemble an upside-down pot!

Pot Rock

The bay is thick o' pots! Toggles and pickup buoys stream in all directions. Panacea hesitates several times as she hitches her way through the labyrinth.

65

Lobster boats prowl the bay, tending pots. How they manage to differentiate, isolate, and access individual buoys and toggles that are so completely jumbled together boggles the mind.

The Independent Man

Cruising friends have offered the use of a mooring off their small island tucked away in Pleasant Bay. Once moored in their idyllic private cove, we are invited ashore for a lobster/crab fest. This is Nirvana, Maine style. Memories of inconvenient encounters with lobster buoys diminish with the flavors of a feast such as this fresh on our palates.

Early the next morning, we cast off the mooring line and thread our way back through a ratted skein of buoy lines. With an outgoing tide, most toggles are in line with their related buoys, making it easier to keep from getting caught between them.

Within an hour we are through the thicket, passing NI, the Nash Island entrance buoy. A squat lighthouse and shed are all that remain of the original buildings on the nearly barren granite knob guarded by the buoy.

We pass through a large mat of seaweed, creating a bizarre swishing sound belowdecks— as if a fan has been switched on.

South of Jonesport, Great Wass and Head Harbor islands waver in fickle fog. This stretch of coast is fairly unpopulated—little but miles of immovable granite and fragrant green spruce. Sizable old swells generate a slow, gentle rocking motion.

Views change dramatically with time because of the 15-foot tidal range here. Places that appear safe at high water reveal dangerous real estate at low. Yellow strands of seaweed spill over purple mussel clumps and flow across jagged ledges into a gentle, lapping sea. Our reality has become eagles soaring overhead and nearby loons eerily crooning to one another. (Spin, web, spin.)

We drop anchor in a small cove off Roque Island Thorofare. Anchorages around Roque Island are plentiful but our choices are limited due to our 6-foot-plus draft. Few other boats are present, most anchoring instead off the spectacular curved sliver of beach rimming the large horseshoe cove north of us.

To the east, a cluster of islands of various shapes and sizes rims Roque Island Harbor.

We are off to Cutler tomorrow. It is always difficult to leave the solitude of Roque. Maybe the fact that we must leave island sanctuaries behind after a few days is what keeps them so special.

68

We set off this morning, relieved there is no fog. Eventually, the though, hazy VLF radio towers of Cutler loom ahead. Our guidebook describes their use for communicating with submarines.

We find plenty of anchoring room inside Cutler's well-protected harbor, complete with a panoramic view of the village houses. Lining the main road parallel to the shore, they squat like little white ducks in a row. Behind us, the ever-hungry fog swallows Little River Island at the entrance. Still ravenous, it swirls onward, soon consuming Panacea and the inner harbor houses. We sit wrapped within a sopping atmospheric dishrag.

After dinner, a sudden clearing surprises us as the fog is momentarily dissipated by an offshore breeze. Just time enough before sunset for a quick sketch of the paper-chain of houses lining the shore.

Western Head stands proud at the southwestern entrance into Cutler Harbor.

The American Lighthouse Foundation has acquired Little River lighthouse and its island from the federal government. Much restoration has been completed, but ongoing maintenance is evidenced by the presence of a ladder to the rooftop. The elements are unkind to these exposed treasures on remote island outposts.

Little River Lighthouse

On departure from Cutler, in good visibility, I quickly sketch the #2 red nun buoy and note its latitude and longitude—might be handy information if conditions are foggy on our return. Just behind the buoy lie reddish-colored nets delineating salmon pens on the eastern side of the harbor. A tangle with them in the fog could certainly ruin one's day, maybe even a couple of days.

The next bright spots of color in our day are the horizontal red bands painted around West Quoddy Head Light on the far shoreline to port. My sketch is long-range, as Sail Rock keeps us from sailing in for a closer view.

A sail past Head Harbour Light on the northeastern tip of Campobello Island leads us into the protection of Head Harbour for the evening. We have sailed into an artist's dream.

The harbor is very tight with fishing boats. Several are tied to barges used for setting up fish weirs, and since there is no room for anchoring, we do the same.

With Panacea secure and her Q flag hoisted, we set off in search of a phone to check in with Canadian customs officials. The mile-long trek into Wilson's Beach and the nearest pay phone gives us a good stretch and makes for a night of sound sleep.

72

The next morning we row out to the lighthouse, landing on a beach exposed for just an hour on either side of low tide. After wading through several inches of floating seaweed to reach the shore, I scramble up the rocks for a quick plein air session, tucking myself off the beaten path for a hasty watercolor. The captain does dinghy watch so we won't become stranded.

Head Harbour
(East Quoddy)
Light

After a few days of touring Campobello, we agree to reverse course on a silver gray morning. Leaves are starting to turn along the shore, and days are crisp. Time to head home, saving parts of the island yet unseen for another time. Inclement weather is forecast for the next few days, and we look forward to hunkering down in the secure and familiar harbor of Cutler.

A final glimpse of Head Harbour lighthouse at high tide reveals no trace of yesterday's landing beach.

Once re-anchored in Cutler Harbor, we are approached by a lobster boat, the Winnifred Hannah. The owner is a former Bermuda One-Two racing competitor of Peter's. Small world! Peter wangles an invitation for lobster fishing the following day.

At 0-dark-hundred the next morning, our fisherman friend pulls alongside and whisks away my captain. I flick on the local VHF working channel and settle in for twelve hours as a lobsterman's wife.

74

Winifred Hannah, Cutler

The men from the sea return in the late afternoon, their boats heard before being seen in heavy mist and rain. The soggy, smelly individual who climbs aboard has gained a huge respect for Maine coast fishermen. I make him disrobe in the cockpit and place his bait-reeking clothing in a garbage bag, where it will ferment until we reach a laundromat.

EAU de LOBSTA'

On a clear, brisk morning following yesterday's frontal passage, we have a great sailing breeze. We raise the main off Little River lighthouse in a 15-knot northwesterly, predicted to increase to 25 knots. We bounce along through old swell.

The rarely seen Libby Island lighthouse is a bold silhouette in bright sun, its horn sounding even though there is no fog today. Old habits die hard.

Libby Island Light

Within two hours the wind has died and we are using the engine. Forecast must have been for a different coast. Half an hour later, the wind returns and we sail again. Nothing is constant!

We have returned to an area of heavy fishing, where lobster buoys abound. In spite of watching closely, we briefly snag a buoy and its toggle with Panacea's fin keel. Luckily, after a few long minutes they slip free. A close one...

We approach Head Harbor, a protected anchorage at Head Harbor Island, lying southeast of Jonesport. Rocks and ledges hide the

Entering the Cows Yard

entrance from sailors approaching from the northeast. One must draw fairly close before the opening becomes apparent. Once inside, an inner harbor called the Cows Yard becomes visible. Strange name for a harbor with nary a cow in sight. Once the anchor is set, we watch as a nearby island breaks into several—its lower portions gradually disappearing on the incoming tide, leaving separate islets. Vivid sunset colors appear as the sun drops behind the new family of islands.

The Cows Yard, High Tide at Sunset

NOT TO BE USED FOR NAVIGATION

NORTHEAST HARBOR, LUNT HARBOR, DEER ISLAND THOROFARE, AND MERCHANT ROW

Northeast Harbor, Lunt Harbor,
Deer Island Thorofare, and Merchant Row

On yet another see-forever, Polartec day, we raise anchor and pick a path between lobster buoys, retracing the channel through the opening alongside Steele Harbor Island. Moose Peak Light on Mistake Island reappears off the starboard bow in incredibly clear visibility.

Once we are around the tip of Mistake Island, the outline of 'tit Manan can again be seen some fifteen miles distant, rare for a lighthouse usually obscured by dense fog.

We pass Crumple Island and its fishermen's shacks to starboard.

Schoodic Point, and Mount Desert Island in the background, grow larger as we slowly close the distance. Wind has dropped off completely. Lobster boats pull their pots on a glassy sea.

Off Schoodic we encounter yet another toggle-and-buoy slalom course of Olympic proportions. Must be a healthy lobster neighborhood below. Behind us, our wake looks like that of a drunken sailor.

A wind shift to the southwest helps us make Northeast Harbor without tacking. After taking on fuel, water, and ice at Clifton Dock, we continue into the harbor and pick up a town mooring for the night.

Picturesque Northeast Harbor is quite a contrast to our previous isolated anchorages. There is much to see and do in this upscale destination port. We spend a peaceful evening in the cockpit, looking up toward the beautiful Asticou Gardens.

Riptide, a resident lobster boat with a pretty little tanbark steadying sail, lies close to the sloop Black Jack, caught earlier by my pencil on our outbound transit.

Riptide, Northeast Harbor

82

We drop our mooring at first light, our only company on departure being lobstermen on their way to work.

Sailing by Southwest Harbor in a southerly direction by Seawall Point, we keep Great Cranberry Island to port as we set our course for Lunt Harbor, Long Island.

Great and Little Duck islands slide by to port.

As we sail along Green Island, an eagle lands on a nearby rocky outcropping, its dark outline contrasting against a bright green carpet surround—a very appropriately named little island.

83

Arriving at Frenchboro, Long Island, we find all moorings occupied, so we drop anchor in the outer harbor. We're ashore within thirty minutes for a walk around the harbor and a visit to the informative island historical society.

Quiet and steady conservation efforts are being made by a farsighted group of individuals diligently working to preserve the quality and appearance of these offshore islands. Long Island has greatly benefited from their tireless efforts.

Although many of the former fishermen's sheds are long gone, there remain a few glimpses of the harbor's original appearance. Lining the long, narrow cove, old docks remain as evidence of a once-active fishing community. While we're there, a day boat pulls up to one such pier, offloading its guests for the afternoon. Struggling for footing on the island roadway, a neatly dressed woman grumbles, "You'd think they'd pave these roads a little better." I want to reply, "Have you taken a traffic count?" but bite my tongue. Some folks will just never get it.

Dinner in the cockpit this evening comes with a five-star view.

View of Frenchboro Waterfront, Lunt Harbor, Long Island

Early morning arrives with a lovely sunrise, lots of high clouds with great mares' tails swishing through a pink and purple palette. The sky has changed from dark to light by adding yellow sun. However, gale winds are forecast for tomorrow, so this is but a treat before the storm.

After a slow start, we make our leisurely way out of Lunt Harbor and around the small islands between Long Island and Swans Island, pulling into the protection of Burntcoat Harbor. We pick up an available mooring just off the dock for easy access ashore when the predicted wind comes up tomorrow.

Burntcoat Harbor

Following a short row to shore, we hike to the lighthouse on Hockamock Head at the harbor entrance.

Spring House at Hockamock Head

Lighthouse Boat Shed

On our return, an elderly gentleman standing alongside the road seems eager for us to stop and visit. Wide barge boards laced with intricate patterns trim the steeply gabled ends of the proud-looking house behind him. He sadly relates that he's had to put the house, along with 300 feet of waterfront and eight acres of land, on the market. His wife is too ill for island living, and he feels too old to continue with lobster fishing. A friend of his sold his home to someone in Pennsylvania over the Internet, so he thinks he'll give it a try too. The islands, now connected to cyberspace, no longer seem so remote. There is something nostalgically sad about this.

We stop at the fishing co-op in the harbor before returning to the boat. A colorful, lazy tabby basks in a patch of sun, blending in with the weather-bleached bench on which it lounges.

87

We linger the next day, while the weather is stomping around with thunder boomers and high winds.

*U*pon leaving Swans Island, we re-enter a world of blue. Picking our way through Toothacher Bay, we continue a motor-sail into Jericho Bay, en route to Deer Island Thorofare. We sail amidst a myriad of island tidbits, scattered about like a broken string of sparkling emeralds. Against the blue sea, a bright red daymark on golden granite Egg Rock completes a colorful primary triad.

*O*nce in the Thorofare, we tick off the island names as they slip by: Eastern Mark Island, Devil and Bold beyond, Grog coming up to starboard, followed by Camp, Russ, and Scott to port.

Grog Island

Scott Island

*M*y attention swings to the large windjammer Mercantile, lying at anchor off Stonington, followed by Crotch Island to port.

Mercantile at anchor

88

At the western entrance of the Thorofare, Mark Island stands proud, its solitary light tower and shed detached from the usual keeper's cottage.

Mark Island
Lighthouse

We drop down into Merchant Row, leaving Wreck, Round, and McGlathery Islands off the port beam as we head around to Harbor Island. In a southwesterly breeze, a natural little harbor there is completely protected by the larger Merchant Island to its south. Harbor Island is one of many well-marked islands monitored by the Maine Island Trail Association, an organization formed to protect island habitats from overuse. An innocent little island, it deserves protection.

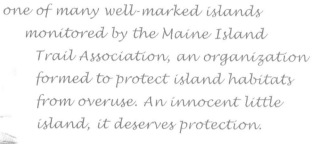

When you're aboard a boat securely anchored at the end of a clear day, just being takes on new meaning. Little matches the seclusion of a peaceful anchorage at sunset. This particular evening is exceptional. Peter softly calls me on deck as I'm below preparing dinner. To the west, a solitary deer has cautiously edged along a granite ledge gradually extending from the Merchant Island shoreline. Behind, two more slowly inch forward as we observe silently, sharing a tenuous moment in time. Silhouettes of the gracefully outlined trio are pasted against a delicate sunset.

90

Hear a Tree Fall...

The experience seems reminiscent of the tree falling in the forest.
Is there sound, if there is no one to hear?
Is there beauty, if there is no one to see?

91

In complete contrast to last evening's solitude, we are awakened at dawn by unmuffled engines as fishing boats roar up and down Merchant Row. Morning rush hour, down east style.

No wind this early as we motor through a lobster-buoy cat's cradle strung over a mirrorlike sea. Little Ewe Island, a granite bit with a crown of pine and spruce, whisks by as we drop down "around the corner" into the Isle au Haut Thorofare.

Ewe Island

House on the Thorofare, Isle au Haut

A strong current quickly moves us past a small cluster of buildings lining the shore. One house in particular catches my eye. Early sunlight streams through the windows from behind while the intense shadow cast by the house seems to ground the structure. The fleeting imprint burns into my memory as I quickly shape some lines.

Isle au Haut lighthouse appears to port, its long, suspended ramp angling back to the keeper's house on Robinson Point.

Within the hour, we are settled at anchor in tiny Duck Harbor on the southwestern shore of Isle au Haut, the only boat present. Unseen ledges and rocks are revealed as the out-going tide drains the basin, the tidal range clearly evident by the number of exposed blocks of granite supporting the nearby landing dock.

13'

Almost hidden by a dense fir thicket, a solitary doe senses no danger as she warily observes from shore. We share her silent security.

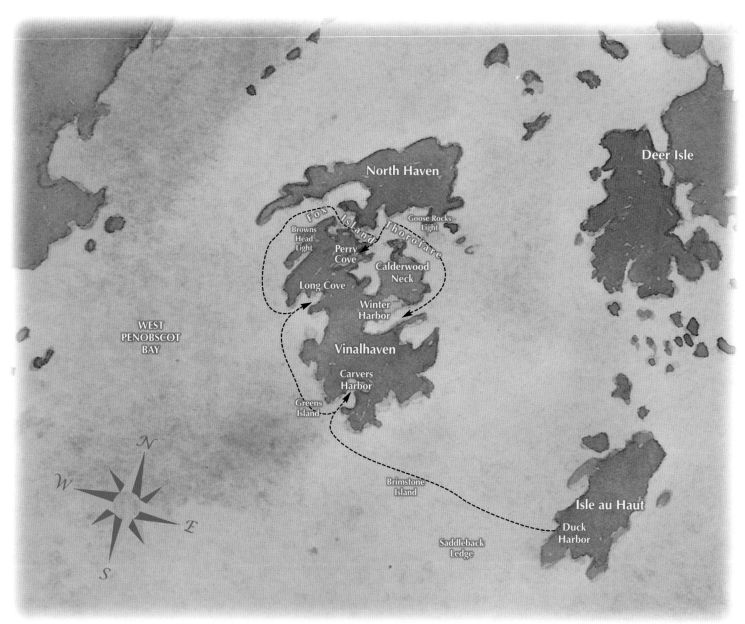

VINALHAVEN AND FOX ISLAND THOROFARE

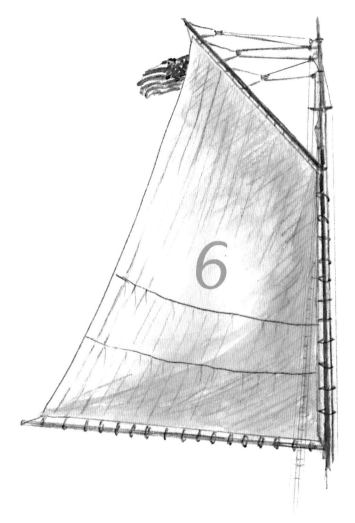

Vinalhaven and
Fox Island Thorofare

A lazy start today, with but a short hop across Isle au Haut Bay
to Carvers Harbor on the "bottom" of Vinalhaven Island.

*S*addleback Ledge and low-lying Brimstone
Island lie below our course to the south.
Several porpoises splash in the waters
around us but seem to be feeding and have
no desire to play with *Panacea's* bow wave.

Saddleback Ledge. The dark little lighthouse
crouches on the ledge, where it warns
great white moths of danger.

*A*t Carvers Harbor, the first empty mooring buoy we retrieve is attached
to a bottle with a note rolled within: "Stay at own risk—$25—must vacate if owner
returns." The message, while considered fair, is not very comforting, so Peter goes
ashore and receives permission to pick up a nearby boatyard rental mooring.

*C*arver is a very
busy, no-nonsense
working harbor.
The fishing docks
are the center of
constant activity. A large herring trawler offloads bait,
which is then transferred to smaller fishing boats in
preparation for early-morning departures. Following
a day at sea, the boats return and offload
their catch at the same dock. Seagulls
and seals compete for the slippery spillage.

96

Fisherman's Shack, Vinalhaven

Ashore, a visit to the informative Vinalhaven Historical Society reveals volumes on the island's early history and granite quarries. As mute testimony to that former industry, nearby Carver Cemetery displays several creative and handsomely carved granite monuments, while an ornate granite watering trough stands at Robert Cassie Square, just beyond.

Our cockpit view this evening. The fleet rests for another busy day tomorrow.

The following dawn, like clockwork, heavy diesels drone as the harvesters of the sea again set off for work. We wait until the harbor is clear to make our leisurely exit, heading around Greens Island at the southwestern tip of Vinalhaven. Remote and picturesque Heron Neck Light sits high atop a clifflike setting on the southern tip of the island.

Heron Neck Lighthouse, Greens Island

Little Hurricane and Hurricane Islands

Little Hurricane

*W*e work our way northward up Hurricane Sound, selecting cozy and secure Long Cove on Vinalhaven as protection from another predicted blow. Anchor well set, Peter is off on a dinghy exploration up the creek while I settle in to capture the calm before the blow. As the tide recedes, hidden ledges are now revealed, rimming the narrow inlet we just navigated. An eagle circles above, the waters are calm, and the sun is bright. The quiet is deafening; the peace, palpable.

Long Cove

*W*e depart Long Cove after a lay day in the rain. Only one other sailor remains at anchor nearby, a college professor from Wisconsin who joins his boat and singlehands in Maine every summer.

*A*s Peter hauls the anchor, the propeller captures a sizeable amount of kelp shaken loose from the anchor chain. Since we are exiting through the narrow ledge-bordered channel, I have no choice but to maintain propulsion. By the time Peter takes over the helm, the prop is solidly wrapped and objecting. No amount of reverse turns would discharge the wad of kelp.

We raise sail in gusty conditions and make our way around to the Fox Island Thorofare, sailing by Browns Head Lighthouse at the western entrance.

Opposite Browns Head lie the Sugar Loaves, a clump of formidable real estate in the middle of the thorofare. We leave them far to port. Lobster buoys are thick around the ledges…must be another popular crustacean hangout.

We pick up a lunch mooring just beyond green daymark 19 and watch as sails billow around the bend, one after another, playing dodge 'em with the North Haven ferry. The resident ospreys atop the marker seem unfazed by the heavy traffic in their vicinity.

101

North Haven Ferry *Captain Neal Burgess*

Angelique

Heritage

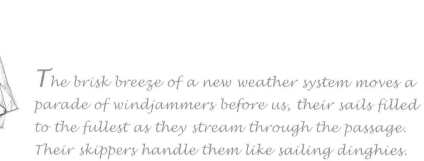

The brisk breeze of a new weather system moves a parade of windjammers before us, their sails filled to the fullest as they stream through the passage. Their skippers handle them like sailing dinghies. We could not have planned a finer lunch program.

J & E Riggin

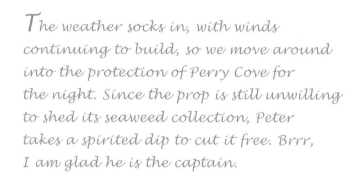

Isaac Evans

The weather socks in, with winds continuing to build, so we move around into the protection of Perry Cove for the night. Since the prop is still unwilling to shed its seaweed collection, Peter takes a spirited dip to cut it free. Brrr, I am glad he is the captain.

Our view is pleasant in spite of overcast skies and chilly temperatures. We retire for the evening and let the wind blow itself out.

Bright and early, we re-enter the Fox Island Thorofare, continuing around Calderwood Point to explore the eastern side of Vinalhaven. I watch with interest as a windjammer sneaks through a skinny passage leading into East Penobscot Bay—definitely only done with local knowledge. As the vessel transits the channel, its gaff mains'l appears to be flying from a spruce-tree mast stepped on a floating island.

Island Under Sail

A serious fishing vessel and several local lobster boats charge by. White and tanbark sails dot the horizon. A veritable potpourri of watercraft join us today.

104

Goose Rocks Light to port marks a nasty patch of water to be avoided. Locally referred to as the Sparkplug, the short, squat light tower does resemble a white goose wearing a black bonnet, although I'm sure the name for the rocks was in use long before the light was placed upon them.

Goose Rocks Light

Windjammers in the Thorofare

Yet another secluded anchorage lies just around Calderwood Neck in Winter Harbor on the northeastern tip of Vinalhaven. Both Vinalhaven and North Haven have a surprising number of protected little gunkholes. A snug and secure anchorage, Winter Harbor is favored for any wind direction except the northeast.

Led by friends in a powerboat with half our draft, Peter takes Panacea in farther than I would. (My captain occasionally navigates as if he's in a shoal-draft dinghy.) My fretting creates stress, so I disappear below. Usually I sit and sketch when nervous, escaping from wherever I am. This time I do not touch a pencil until the anchor is safely set. Give me deep offshore ocean over shores with skinny waters and hidden ledges!

A granite roadblock off the bow rivets my attention when I emerge from below. This massive impediment is visible at high tide; at low it expands. It would make a profitable property investment in today's real estate market.

Things That Go Bump

A Room with a View

*Although probably undesirable
from within, this shack makes
an interesting study from my
current vantage point.*

*The view looking back out to the bay is unparalleled:
a slide show of graceful windjammers in a continually changing
diorama as they glide across Winter Harbor's narrow entrance.*

Surprise

Olad

*Once settled in, it is as if we are on
a landlocked lake, and we share a
peaceful evening with friends.*

J & E Riggin

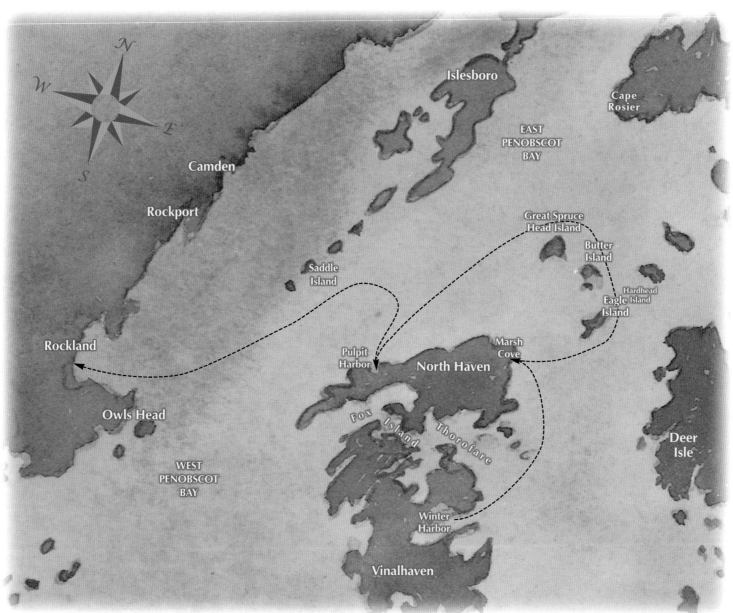

NORTH HAVEN, EAST PENOBSCOT BAY ISLANDS, AND ROCKLAND HARBOR

North Haven, East Penobscot Bay Islands,
and Rockland Harbor

On our exit the next morning, I again dive below,
coward that I am, as Peter reverses our inbound course
and safely guides Panacea back around ledges and mussel
shoals. My sketchbooks would not be nearly as interesting
were it not for his adventuresome spirit. During these
moments, I must constantly remind myself of this.
My mantra, "Nothing is constant," gets me through.

Leaving Fox Island Thorofare to port, we head
to the northeastern tip of North Haven and
drop anchor in pretty little Marsh Cove.

Hog Island

Hog Island, complete with a huge osprey nest, forms a natural
breakwater. Oak, Burnt, Dagger, Downfall, and Sheep islands lie
between us and a hazy blue Deer Isle on the eastern horizon.

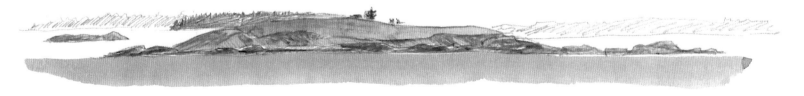

Dagger Island

When we awake the next morning, a family of ducks quacks by in flat, calm waters. Off the beam, a reflective puddle of blue encircles Hog Island and its osprey nest.

Bald Island

Once the wind builds, we raise sail and slowly wander north, passing Bald Island and the Porcupines on our way to Eagle Island.

Porcupine Islands

We skirt around the lighthouse and bell tower on Eagle Island's northeast point. Fortunately, the light escaped demolition when a government team tore down the keeper's house in 1964 as a cost-saving measure. The tower remains badly scarred where the house was torn away.

Continuing northwest of Eagle Island, we anchor briefly off Butter Island while Peter retrieves a floating piece of driftwood for a future wood turning project. At times our decks resemble those of an old lumber schooner, bearing the weight of salvaged planks, tree stumps, and any other wood oddment deemed "turnable."

A young couple aboard a tidy little lobster boat tend a string of pots to port, their young child contentedly observing the work ethic of the sea.

Hardhead Island lies to the east, with a pale backdrop of Deer Isle beyond.

Eagle Island Light

*U*nder way once more, we round Butter Island along its northern shore, sailing past Great Spruce Head Island, Beach Island, and Colt Head, followed by Resolution and Horse Head islands.

*N*othing but islands, windjammers, and Camden's blue hills—always and everywhere, windjammers and rolling, faded-blue hills.

Nathaniel Bowditch

Lewis R. French

Timberwind

*P*ulpit Harbor on North Haven Island will be our final anchorage of this cruise. We plan to sit out another weak frontal system, this being an ideal place to do so. Clouds have continued to build throughout the day, and skies appear more menacing as we drop sail and motor through the entrance, passing yet another resident osprey nest.

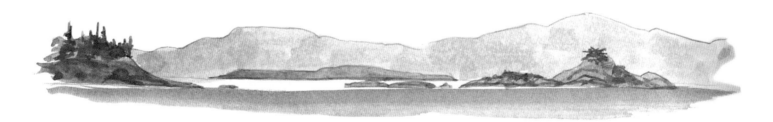

*O*nce settled in, we watch windjammers race through the harbor entrance, hoping to beat the impending deluge. Peter dinghies me over for a sketch of the ancient osprey nest.

*T*he evening is spent hunkered below as the heavens let loose. We are in a warm and dry cocoon immersed in water.

116

In the early morning, we drowsily hear the clanking cadence of anchor chain being winched aboard. Within thirty minutes, the entire fleet of windjammers sails into a gray gauze of fog swallowing the bay. We are reminded of how lucky we are to be free of any time schedule.

FogBound VICTORY CHIMES   M.S.McCrea

Victory Chimes

Composition by Nature

Composition by Nature   M.S.McCrea

I sketch and paint while we bide our time here. I have a small watercolor almost completed when a droplet of condensation falls from the boom and lands in the center of my painting's sky. Ruined, I think. However, when the painting dries, the droplet imprint resembles a hazy orb of sun. The small watercolor has named itself—a title determined by fate.

117

A New Day, Pulpit Harbor—
Dealer's Choice and *Wendameen*

Thunderstorms rumble throughout the night, leaving behind a morning so clear and crisp its colors are snapping. Reflections are so pure it is as if our world is upside down and we are floating on the sky. The blue hills from the west leap from a crystalline, ice blue sea. A resident lobsterboat courteously departs at low throttle. The crew aboard Wendameen do a daily deck swash in spite of the rains. All these sights are duly noted and spun away in the web.

On a nearby anchored boat, the parents of a young girl launch a sailing pram with a colorful tanbark spritsail. Her father rigs the boat and sets the confident young lady on her way. Pondering the peaceful start of a new day, we watch as she gingerly guides her craft in a fickle morning breeze. Oh, that every child could share an experience such as this at least once in a lifetime.

Triple Sprit Sail

119

Flying Fish, a pretty black schooner, sails in and out on a brief harbor tour.

Sailing in...

Sailing out...

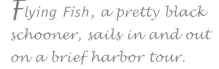

*L*ate in the afternoon we leave Pulpit Harbor. The captain stretches every last minute of the cruise. Sailing parallel to the mainland along the island chain south of Islesboro, we see the profile of Saddle Island repeated in the mountain range behind Camden. Nature continues to supply me with inspirational journal entries.

*T*he familiar outline of the Rockland Breakwater Light appears on the horizon, growing larger on our approach. Our world of blue will soon turn green. We ride individual waves of thought as images sail by.

Morning in Maine tacks toward Owls Head Light

Far from
Madding Crowds

Lighthouse lovers stroll the breakwater.
Some clamber over the lighthouse balcony
in an effort to get closer to the sea, while
others sit below on the rocks, soaking up
the quiet. Similar to cruising, being at
this isolated outpost makes one feel
far from the madding crowds.

The Vinalhaven Ferry Returning
to Rockland Harbor

Stephen Taber

121

Whenever a cruise such as this draws to a close, I suffer the obligatory moment of reverse panic. When we set out, I needed time to settle into the pace of a sailor's days, to leave mainland cares behind. Now, as we return, I wonder if I'm ready to rejoin the hectic pace of shore-side living. Whether we are making a fifteen-month Atlantic Circle voyage or a two-week getaway, the releasing and retying of land connections and commitments are always the most difficult aspects of a cruise.

No matter how difficult the transitions, however, our relaxed memories will remain readily available; a glimpse into the filled pages of my journal will assure that peaceful reflections of our Maine sail can always be evoked. And, should they fade, an ever-ready Panacea is waiting to take us on another cruise.

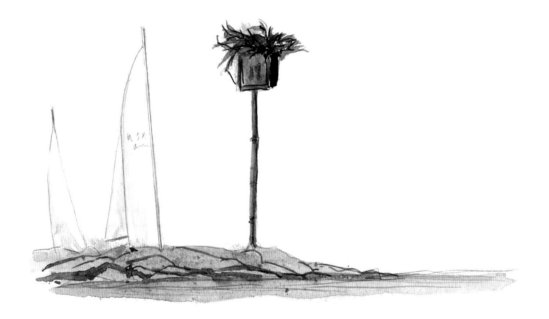

Appendixes

PARTICULARS OF THE SAILING VESSEL
PANACEA

Freedom 32
LOA: 32'9"
LWL: 25'9"
Beam: 12'3"
Draft: 6'1"

Peter selected the name *Panacea*. At the time, he was enmeshed in the world of applied physics and chemistry of industrial R&D, his profession that of constantly searching for the perfect panacea.

Panacea is a Freedom 32, a cat sloop auxiliary sailing yacht, hull #35. The boat was designed by Garry Hoyt and built by Tillotson-Pearson, Inc., of Warren, R.I., in 1984. Peter is her original owner. She has a fin keel forward of a spade rudder and powers with a 22-horsepower Yanmar diesel driving a 2-bladed Martec propeller. The engine charges four 12-volt batteries with a 125-amp alternator. A

Remember Home. *Panacea* leaving Pulpit Harbor

32-gallon aluminum fuel tank lies amidships beneath a settee. The freestanding carbon fiber mast is keel stepped and has no standing rigging. Her sail inventory includes a fully battened main with three sets of reefing points, a 100-square-foot working jib, a light-air staysail for reaching, a twin jib (designed for downwind sailing), and a spinnaker, flown from the 18-foot yard centered on the bow pulpit.

Added equipment includes a Monitor self-steering system and an Autohelm 3000 auto-pilot; Furuno 1621 radar; Apelco 6000 Loran; Micrologic ML250 GPS; anemometer; VHF and SSB radios. For anchors, she carries a Bruce 33, a Danforth 20H, Danforth 12H, and a Fortress 23. A Muir manual windlass is installed on the foredeck to help with retrieval of 100 feet of 5/16 BBB chain.

The galley has a double stainless steel sink, an ice chest good for nine days, and a two-burner, gimbaled, Force 10 propane stove. Water is stored in a 50-gallon tank beneath a starboard settee and an 18-gallon tank forward. A watermaker is aboard for offshore passages. A Force 10 propane heater in the main salon/dinette area takes the nip off early spring and late fall sails. A standing nav station, two staterooms, and an aft head with shower (or hatch opening for sun shower), and a wet gear lock complete the accommodations below deck.

A hatch-dodger covers the staircase-like companionway, leading from below to a commodious cockpit. A Sunbrella bimini can be extended over the full length of the cockpit for UV protection. An inflatable dinghy with a 4-horsepower outboard is towed along as a go-ashore taxi.

All in all, *Panacea* is the perfect boat for us. She's taken us by castles in Spain and to gunkholes in Maine. She has shown herself to be a comfortable and dependable cruiser, while at the same time remaining competitive as a single-handed offshore racer in her class. She has proven herself by taking several first- and second-place class finishes in six biennial Bermuda One-Two Races, her most recent in June 2003. To date, the vessel and her skipper have logged 51,000 sea miles.

GLOSSARY

Bermuda One-Two	A biennial two-legged off-shore race from Newport, Rhode Island, to St. George, Bermuda, in which the skipper solos a boat to Bermuda on a 635-mile rhumb line course (first leg) and returns to Newport with one additional crew member (second leg)
Coasters	A nineteenth-century term for schooners built for coastal trade
Day mark or daybeacon	An unlighted fixed navigation aid marking submerged ledges or other hazards
Down east	Since the prevailing wind along coastal Maine is from the southwest, vessels heading eastward are usually sailing downwind, hence down east. In that sense, down east always refers to some place farther east than where one happens to be at the time, but the phrase has also become synonymous with the Maine coast region, though exactly where

	"the real down east" begins remains a matter for debate.
Draft	The depth of water required to float a vessel
Gunkhole	A small, protected cove well off the beaten track, where sailors on a leisurely cruise can find a quiet anchorage.
Head boat	Any boat for hire to take passengers for day trips or week-long excursion
Hook	Another term for a vessel's anchor
Lay day/ layover	An additional, unplanned day spent in port or at anchor
Lobster buoys	Styrofoam or wooden floats attached to the pot warp (rope or line) connected to lobster traps
Mooring	A semipermanent anchor (often a chunk of granite, in Maine) on the sea floor attached by

	chain and line (tackle) to a float on the surface
Navigation aids	Fixed and floating marks and buoys, including lighthouses, set to warn of hazards to navigation or to mark safe channels
Panacea	A supposed remedy or cure-all, usually elusive
Plein air	Painting in the open air (fr)
Port	Nautical term for anything on the left side of the vessel, looking forward
Q Flag	The signal flag for the letter Q (i.e., quarantine), which must be flown until customs clearance has been secured
Singlehand	To sail alone on a type of boat or in a situation usually handled by more than one person
Starboard	Nautical term for anything on the right side of the vessel, looking forward
Swell	Long undulations of water moving along the sea surface —usually an old wave train from a distant vigorous weather system
Tanbark sails	Sails dyed with tannin, a dark red coloring derived from leaves and bark; the color today is duplicated in sails made from synthetics
Thick o' fog	Heavy fog conditions; way down east, in Nova Scotia, it's sometimes pronounced "tik-o-fog"